Also by David Lehman

POETRY

The Daily Mirror

Valentine Place

Operation Memory

An Alternative to Speech

NONFICTION

The Last Avant-Garde:
The Making of the New York School of Poets

The Big Question

The Line Forms Here

Signs of the Times:
Deconstruction and the Fall of Paul de Man

The Perfect Murder: A Study in Detection

EDITED BY DAVID LEHMAN

The Best American Poetry (series editor)

The KGB Bar Book of Poems (with Star Black)

Ecstatic Occasions, Expedient Forms:
85 Leading Contemporary Poets Select and Comment on Their Poems

James Merrill:
Essays in Criticism (with Charles Berger)

Beyond Amazement:
New Essays on John Ashbery

# The Evening Sun

A Journal in Poetry

DAVID LEHMAN

SCRIBNER POETRY

NEW YORK   LONDON   TORONTO   SYDNEY   SINGAPORE

SCRIBNER POETRY
1230 Avenue of the Americas
New York, NY 10020

SCRIBNER POETRY and design are trademarks of Macmillan Library Reference USA, Inc.,
used under license by Simon & Schuster, the publisher of this work.

For information regarding special discounts for bulk purchases,
please contact Simon & Schuster Special Sales at 1-800-456-6798 or
*business@simonandschuster.com*

DESIGNED BY ERICH HOBBING

Manufactured in the United States of America

1   3   5   7   9   10   8   6   4   2

Library of Congress Cataloging-in-Publication Data
Lehman, David, 1948–
The evening sun : a journal in poetry / David Lehman.
p.  cm.
I. Title.

PS3562.E428 E94 2002
811'.54—dc21    2001057569

ISBN 0-7432-2552-X

*for Stacey Harwood*

To write a journal in verse, not only for personal pleasure but for public consumption, is to turn a journalistic form—the daily dispatch from the front—into a poetic one. Writing *The Evening Sun* I sometimes felt as if I were creating a poetry newspaper that my father could read on the subway ride home from the office if my father were still alive and people still depended on the afternoon paper for late scores and early market returns. I was (and still am) inspired by the idea of journalism in this double sense. On the one hand, I could keep in mind models of poetry journals on the order of A. R. Ammons's *Tape for the Turn of the Year*. On the other hand, I *had* worked in journalism for a period of years, and though I could never quite overcome the feeling that I was impersonating a journalist, something must have rubbed off, because there is an element of reportage in at least some of these poems and the emphasis is very deliberately on communication.

Like *The Daily Mirror*, its predecessor, *The Evening Sun* consists of 150 of the poems I wrote after embarking on the project of writing a poem a day. I'd had so much fun with *The Daily Mirror* that I didn't want to give up the habit when I turned in the manuscript in January 1999. The new poems I was writing quickly persuaded me that a sequel covering the turn of the century was under way. The image of "the evening sun" recurred before I realized how apt a title it made, completing a night-and-day symmetry and evoking (as *The Daily Mirror* had done) a defunct New York newspaper, in this case the New York *Sun*. As a result of mergers the *Sun* survived in my childhood as the New York *World Telegram & Sun*, which was in fact my father's afternoon paper until it died, a casualty of either a calamitous newspaper strike or the hegemony of the new media as Marshall McLuhan understood it.

I am aware of raising several other echoes with my title. A James Schuyler poem called "Song" in his book *The Morning of the Poem* begins with these evocative lines: "The light lies layered in the leaves. / Trees, and trees, more trees. / A cloud boy brings the evening paper: / *The Evening Sun*. It sets." As I type these words Jo Stafford is singing "St. Louis Blues," which protests the setting of the sun. If a melancholy note creeps into these pages it's because I, too, hate to see that evening sun go down.

There is nothing random about the selection of poems. I chose these 150 because I felt they were the best poems in the best order and formed a unity greater than the sum of its parts. The chief conceit is that the twelve months of the year correspond to the twelve chapters of a book. Accordingly we move with the circular logic of the seasons from New Year's Day to the day presidents are inaugurated, from St. Valentine's Day to the opening day of baseball season, from Hurricane Floyd in September 1999 to an October 2000 presidential debate between two candidates here identified as "Gush" and "Bore" and from Halloween and the changing of the clocks back to New Year's Eve. There is plenty of time for personal obsessions to emerge along the way, and the recurrent subjects here include the movies in general, Hitchcock in particular, the style and implications of *noir*, the fortunes of the New York Mets and Knicks, love, sex, jazz, art, the stock market, the twentieth century, World War II, the 1960s, my son Joe, *Hamlet,* Wallace Stevens, and the city of New York. Most of these poems were written in New York, some in Ithaca, New York, some in Bennington, Vermont, and some on the road in hotel rooms or friends' houses in Houston, Tulsa, Savannah, Chicago, Boston, the Napa Valley, Vienna, Los Angeles, Paris, Miami, and Paterson, New Jersey.

When Joe was five he didn't say I'm hungry
he said I feel the hungriness and later that late August day
the hottest in years he gathered the fallen leaves
and pasted them back on the trees I felt like that
today like Joe at five or the tourist in paradise whose
visa has expired the revolution has begun the junta
has shut down the airport there's no escape so here I'll say
goodbye to the other children I knew when we were
children, skating at the edge of the pond, I didn't specially
want it to happen, this change in the clock calendar century
I just wanted things to continue as they had, do I sound like
a jilted lover no you sound like yourself and I'm here I'm hearing
everything twice everything twice a saxophonist a trumpet
and then a singer lifts me with soft lights and sweet music
and you in my arms let's be like the boy at five who
said he wanted to be a ghost when he grew up but
grew up to celebrate the marriage of flesh and air
in a lonely place with paranoid Bogart and Gloria
Grahame the director's wife that's poetry noir for you
champagne cocktails with blood orange juice and
then to eat with a hearty appetite feeling the hungriness

There's an astronaut named David Lehman
an authority on South American politics
and at least one soldier who died in Vietnam
I saw his name on the Vietnam Memorial
and who should phone me on this day
but a woman who claims she's married to me
and apologizes when I tell her she's not
she's a wrong number I shall long cherish
I assure her wondering which David Lehman
was or is her husband
On the first day of school when I was six
the principal called my name I stood up
and said there were two David Lehmans
maybe he didn't mean me
but he did it was my lucky day which
reminds me of the movie we saw on January 1st
*Christmas in July* with Dick Powell
"Is it good luck or bad luck if a
black cat crosses your path?"
"It depends on what happens after"
and "If you don't sleep at night it
isn't the coffee it's the bunk"

## To Mercury

I wasn't a trickster but the joker
in the deck the wild card not a
con man but the prankster who poured salt
and pepper into the coach's coffee when
his back was turned, not the goldfish-swallowing
how many can fit into a phone booth
collegiate 50s but the Johnny Carson
meets Bob Dylan 60s and off they go
to see Tippi Hedren in *Marnie* and *The Birds*
not a veteran with a flair for gallows humor
but a boy convinced of his perpetual youth
lived with a perpetual muse and this is my day
this is Hermes' day as he delivers his letters
and messages to each, spreading the world
the bread the brain the panic the pain
the Indians were right to refuse to let
the photographers steal their image
but the joke was on us with our cameras
we wanted the world to stay as it was
with grown-ups remaining the age they were
while we children grew stronger and older, and soon
we couldn't recognize anything seen
in the window the mirror or the little screen

The wind does whistle but it also hums
if you say it does, because you have
that power: language makes it possible,
and you have the choice: you can revile
the slogans and shibboleths of groupthink
or you can watch TV commercials as if
they were aesthetic products to be
appreciated and analyzed: not much
of a choice, is it: let's go beyond
"either/or" and see if we can't just ignore
what offends our nostrils, and make
something out of our minds, out of our
minds in both senses: let's see
what happens when the imagination as
conceived by Wallace Stevens marries
the language as conceived by millions daily

# JANURY 9

JANUARY 9

∞

## PRESS CONFERENCE

Gentlemen, this is my last press conference
I know how he felt, he was on to them
but they were on to him too he knew the rules
before he felt free to break them but this
was worse this was nihilism with a human farce
the bastards he'd beat them yet some remain obscure
some are obscure and later become popular
some posthumously some never if everyone
says you're no good you could be great
or no good some look at what's there and see
what isn't which makes them either visionaries,
ex-eulogists for Robert F. Kennedy, or dupes
of doubletalk who have seen the future
and know it's a basket full of discarded documents
some quit some conquer their appetite
and thus achieve the desired thinness

Time with an insolent
toothpick in his mouth
asks a stranger for the time
the stranger is a woman
wearing rouge à lèvres
and boucles d'oreilles
because we're in Paris
and she asks
Do you play piano?
and he says
No, I play attitude piano
that's the way it goes
unlike hateful married life
where he feels angry she feels guilty
she says she's sorry he doesn't give a damn
and hours go by before the remorse code
is deciphered, repealed

In school I studied
the window, years
changed, forward or back,
before I understood
the concept of time,
which seemed like
a truth at the time
but now seems a major
falsehood but only
because I am studying
the window, which is
the same window as
when I was a boy

∞

When Robert Frost recited "The Gift Outright"
in the gleaming cold noonday sun I was watching
there was no school I don't remember why
that afternoon we played touch football, my friends and I
on a sloping meadow in Fort Tryon Park
and life was going on elsewhere, life was going on downtown
in night clubs that even then were going out of fashion
like the Stork Club or El Morocco and my friends and I
wanted to grow up and smoke cigarettes and drink highballs
and buy fur coats for our wives and take them to clubs
because that was life, and what we didn't realize
was that our afternoon in Fort Tryon Park
where we got into a fight with some Irish kids
was also life and even then was turning
into history with the Bay of Pigs and the Vienna Summit
and Berlin and the missile crisis and the speech in Berlin
and the discotheques that put the night clubs out of business
and Sam Giancana, the mob boss who would have
ordered a hit on Sinatra except he wanted
to hear him sing "Chicago" one more time

## INSTANT MESSAGE

Art is that which can be
interrupted John Cage
said according to David
Shapiro in Instant Message
mode his son is taking Advanced
Biology (we called it sex)
how sweet, as a harlot said
to Baudelaire I asked how
he said "not sure, as
Wittgenstein said about
the presence of rhinos in his room"
and Cage praised silence
than which nothing could be more
theatrical except maybe the evening
sun that never goes down
"layered in light like leaves"
and on the day he (Cage) died the kids
said to me the guy you're always
quoting is dead I said who who who
the guy you're quoting is always dead

## ODE TO MODERN ART

Come on in and stay a while
I'll photograph you emerging from the revolving door
like Frank O'Hara dating the muse of modern art
Talking about the big Pollock show is better
than going to it on a dismal Saturday afternoon
when my luncheon partner is either the author or the subject
of *The Education of Henry Adams* at a hard-to-get-
a-table-at restaurant on Cornelia Street
just what is chaos theory anyway
I'm not sure but it helps explain "Autumn Rhythm"
the closest thing to chaos without crossing the border
I think you should write that book on Eakins and also the one
on nineteenth-century hats the higher the hat the sweller the toff
and together we will come up with Mondrian in the grid
        of Manhattan
Gerald Murphy's "Still Life with Wasp" and the best Caravaggio
        in the country
in Kansas City well it's been swell, see you in Cleveland April 23
The reason time goes faster as you grow older is that each day
is a tinier proportion of the totality of days in your life

## Poem Noir

Sex wasn't a digression
It was the destination
The plot begins in awe
ends in failure
and is filmed in black and white
with Barbara Stanwyck
At the bars, Marxism was out
Existentialism was in
and their preferred form of escapism was
death penalty news & updates
a trumpet solo
the record spinning
the needle moving
two cigarettes in the ashtray
and this prayer I make to thee
O Love deliver me from evil
with skin wounds only
and Lee Wiley's voice
"for I don't stand a ghost
of a chance with you"

Nothing extends a phone
call more effectively than
saying you're on your way out
but she wants to tell you
the five things she requires
in a man one is intelligence
he must have a brain
also he must be good a term
she likes because it embraces both
the opposite of evil and "good in
bed" and you admire the way
she skillfully maneuvered the
conversation to the sex lives
of jazz fans who live in the Village
and the enduring validity
of the Cyrano story and so
well you wish you didn't have to go

Diann Blakely doesn't have the flu
she has flu noir
and Star Black is star noir
Rebecca Livingston contributes
her "comfortable ass clicking garments"
and whoever wears them knows
life is comedy noir in a good mood
but the way I feel right now is
thanks for phoning me, bitch
you're no English muffin yourself, lady
George Steinbrenner
is as frightened of the Mets
as Nixon was of the brothers Kennedy
everyone had relatives at 1127 Vice Avenue
in the Bronx & the greater the sense
of sin the greater the climax

### Sculpture Garden (Houston)

David Smith made
*Two Circle Sentinel*
in 1961 he was 55
and used stainless steel
scratched so it would catch
the light as it does a
student comes along says
he used a grinder to get that
effect he (the student) knows
from welding school you half
expect it to spring into
semaphore meanwhile in
bronze there's a Maillol nude
in the voluptuous Kim Novak
in *Vertigo* manner which I
prefer to the gymnast heroines
of Robert Graham impressive
as they are their hard lean
bodies sculpted in 1983
the Maillol in 1910 & between
them came the pill
and changed the definition of beauty

## The Business

They could be anyone's opinions
fights, frustrations, likes and dislikes,
victories and defeats, love letters, class notes, tall tales,
they could belong to everyone but they happen to be mine
today yours tomorrow like a book like a box of books
the store ordered but has the right to return so
from the publisher's point of view it's as if they're gone
today here tomorrow that's the nature of the business
of words their manufacture and distribution
from factory to warehouse a few months
on a shelf a few hours in somebody's lap
open to page 142 when he fell asleep
but it lives on in his dreaming mind

### Portrait d'une Femme

She had the ugliest handwriting
and the prettiest green eyes
of any woman at the Museum
of Modern Art. She had
the loveliest legs and the smallest
apartment of any editor
at *Vogue.* She had the reddest
hair and the worst insomnia
of any actress on the Upper West Side.
She had the best mind and
the nastiest manners of any Swarthmore
graduate in the gym. She had
the meanest father and the leanest
mother and the crudest brother
and the lewdest sister and the most
money and the least compunction
of any divorcee in this room.
She had the sweetest voice.
She had the darkest moods.

Patricia Highsmith said
neither life nor nature
gives a damn about justice
which is why it "amuses" her
to see people get outraged
at crimes she likes the villain
who is cunning and brave
gets away & won't knuckle
under to the boring boring
ghastly predictable workings
of the justice machine in
neoclassical palaces in
European cities when she
would rather be in Venice
on the water where disaster
and sexuality and murder
hide in the alleys where it's
impossible not to get lost

They now call
downtown New York
where astronauts and generals
and winners of the World Series
parade in convertibles and
are showered with ticker tape
the "canyon of heroes"
a great phrase
that I shall use
for the canal zone between
your lovely lithe legs

That's what I like to see
A cab pulling up a woman getting out
and heading straight for this table
She says: Let's say I came fifteen minutes late
Would you be mad at me?
He says: No
She says: How about thirty minutes?
And when she does come she says
I'm late because I thought you'd be later
She's wearing velvet pants, deep purple,
and the greatest high heels in SoHo
She will let him invest her money
if he lets her design his apartment
is it a deal? it's a deal
and she smiles when he says
you're looking very Lady tonight

The cigarette is to the dream
as the night to the evening light
after sunset when the sun
is still smiling on the part
of the world where I am not
and I who belong to Generation T
(which was once the cutting edge,
three consonants and a vowel ago)
use ink and eraser fluid to draw
a blank, red at the light, green
in the distance, amber in the splendor
of dusk with air still fresh though night
so old has lost all stars but one
the one that will rise for me at dawn

## ISSUES

I had issues with the pronouns in the other lines, too.
It started to kick in for me with the part about the war.
Did what I say make sense to you?

I wondered whether what "you" said was true,
Which may have been what "you" were aiming for.
I had issues with the pronouns in the other lines, too,

And not just the pronouns but the branding ("Mountain Dew").
I like the imagery especially "in the forest there's a door."
Did what I say make sense to you?

But I wish the poem didn't dodge the repercussions of "Jew,"
And I winced at "hoodlums and whores."
I had issues with the pronouns in the other lines, too,

But in the other lines what comes through is you,
What I hear is your voice, a kind of quiet roar.
Did what I say make sense to you?

Don't get me wrong, I like the second-person point of view,
But it raises issues. Like what. Like gender.
I had issues with the pronouns in the other lines, too.
Did what I say make sense to you?

If you were a monkey's uncle
and I were the monkey who wrote *Hamlet*
I'd explain why Wallace Stevens
is Keats on acid but then
we'd be back in the century of no return
and you'd turn into Lot's wife
and I'd follow the angels blindly
after washing their feet I'd hear
the explosions behind us and I'd picture
them a deep gash vermillion in the sky
red as a desert each poem a time
capsule meant to pop open on some
unspecified future day which will come
as surely as triple witching hour
on select Fridays on Wall Street
when all the options expire

## Bar Association

I didn't mean to alarm you
When I told you I loved you
I thought it would charm you
I was drunk at the time

When I told you I loved you
You wore pristine blue jeans at the bar
I was drunk at the time
Don't think I didn't notice

You wore pristine blue jeans at the bar
And sat on the bar stool beside me
Don't think I didn't notice
And the predicted snow began to fall

You sat on the bar stool beside me
When you looked in the mirror it dissolved
And the predicted snow began to fall
But failed to accumulate, disappointing all

When you looked in the mirror it dissolved
When you looked out the window it snowed
But failed to accumulate, disappointing all
Who had stayed awake to watch it fall

When you looked out the window it snowed
And the moon was full
We had stayed awake to watch it fall
And day broke

And the moon was full
I thought it would charm you
And day broke
I didn't mean to alarm you

I was a child he took me aside said
you've got a lot going for you
doubt, for one thing
you communicate doubt
as effectively as fickle freshmen
communicate illness
in their hospitable beds
and doubt is big this year
doubt is in, it's the condition
we're in, man,
and you mastered it
before you turned twenty-one
you had it mastered when
what you wanted to master
was nudity and Yale
you didn't know then how much
more fruitful is the world you mastered
of doubt
which you doubt

They asked me to define you
O Irony what shall I say
shall I describe writing
a meticulous courteous
bread-and-butter note
to someone one loathes
loathing the person more
with each word no that's
probably not a good example
Irony you are less a rhetorical
figure or a dramatic device than
a way of knowing what Desdemona
doesn't about her destiny but also
Irony is going to the second act
missing the first and Irony is
the woman I am taking to the theater
funny I didn't expect you
to have dark hair brown eyes
but now I've met you I can't recall
the image of you I had before

## THE LIFT

The wonderful thing
about being with
you in this hotel
lift in London full
of people is that none
of them knows what
you and I are about to do
in bed or possibly
on the floor in fact not
even you realize yet
how much you're going
to enjoy this act for
which we have no name
not clinical or hideous, just
a double-digit number, perfect
as a skater's figure eight

I don't know about the catalogue copy of my book
On the phone I read it to Bill who says
it could be a major motion picture what a hook
high concept with Tom Hanks as John Ashbery
and Kevin Spacey as Frank O'Hara we're having
trouble casting the other two and Bill thinks I should
go with the Matt Damon generation while my mind
turns naturally to the long-deceased Montgomery
Clift as the young James Schuyler but who would
play Professor Wizard alias Kenneth Koch and who
Jane Freilicher cracking wise as Robert de Niro
playing Larry Rivers pursues her in *Mean Streets*
with Gerry Mulligan on sax this is rapidly
turning into my poem of the day, Bill, and I wish
I could join you at Pravda with the rest of the cast
(regards to Jaye tell her to get well fast)

Every so often my father comes over
for a visit he hangs his overcoat and hat
on my hat rack I brief him on recent
developments and serve us coffee
he is surprised that I like to cook
once when he made an omelette
he flipped it in the air much to my delight
and it landed on the floor yes that
was the summer of 1952, he remembered
the high breakers and how fearless
I was running into the ocean anyway
the important thing is to see you doing
so well he said and took his coat and hat
and left before I remembered he was dead

We who dress
conventionally do so
because we're secretly
weirder than you
and afraid you'll
find us out.
"Sorry I'm late."
"What happened?" "I
almost got stuck
in traffic." "I
thought you went
on foot." "Did
I come at
a bad time?"
"Well, we're just
having a divorce."
This is America.
The psychiatrists are
certifiable. The security
guards wear sweatshirts:
"Nixon's the One."

They were wrong
for whom success
was sweetest. It's
failure that interests
me. It's why
I like movies
that look like
they were filmed
down under the
Manhattan Bridge overpass
a raw March
Sunday, warehouses empty,
black and white
and always 1953,
and the hero
believes in nothing
like the waiter
in Hemingway who
prays to nada
our nada who
art nada nada
be thy name

All the songs this morning
rhyme spring with birds
on the wing Sarah Vaughan
Carmen McRae and Sinatra
wishful thinking what else
is poetry and we know it's
coming like caffeine I wish
I were waking up with you
this morning as my sinuses
adjust to the dust and smoke
of New York with cream and
sugar I bought a small painting
yesterday with the letters B,
E, and G in it not the beggar's
art but the beginning of a day
like that of a season when
the change is too gradual
to notice but one day it's here

In New York where the subway lines
have letters the R and the N
stand for the Rarely and Never
the D is for desultory, dreary
the E for every time I missed it
the F for the folks who live in Forest Hills
the B and the C for Bare and Clothed
and the A is for Duke Ellington
of course whereas London has
the Circle line, the Piccadilly line
the Northern line, the Victoria line,
the Bakerloo, the Metropolitan, etc.
each has a color of its own
as in Boston they have the red line
which goes to Harvard Square
once when I was there
a friend called it Red Square
by mistake but I could see his point

The first time I read
Wallace Stevens's poem
"Esthetique du Mal"
I misread it
I read
"the greatest poetry
is not to live
in a physical world"
when what he wrote
was "the greatest
poverty is not
to live in a
physical world"
with globes of fruit
on the table or a bunch
of bananas and blue
grapes in a crystal bowl

I'm taking jazz as
a second language
in jazz if you have *chops*
it means you can do things
with your right hand like Art
Tatum at the piano while people
at the bar keep talking not
realizing you're Art Tatum
and later when we play the song
we like the fact that we can
hear their chatter indistinct
in the background as he jumps
around the keyboard with
such quick elegance like a dance
of fingers and keys
now with a singer you don't
say *chops* you say *pipes*
as in the case of Sarah Vaughan
who could do things with her
voice that no one heard
until she did them, and not even then

The longer I stare the lovelier
you look in my eyes (so made such
mirrors and spies) and I'm not done
yet as I enumerate the virtues
of your smile, gracious in defeat,
victorious in love, your breasts
and belly and below, the zone I'd
like to zone in on, your ankles
unshod, your brassiere and panties
strewn on the floor, you are
my Psyche (Greek for memory or soul)
and I will visit your sleep tonight
you won't see me but I'll be there
beside you for hours and when
you wake in my arms I will kiss
your eyes shut and then kiss you more

I know a good zeugma
(or syllepsis) when I hear
one and when Keely Smith
singing "Angel Eyes" just now
got to "The drink and the laugh's
on me" that's it I thought
the heartbreak behind the rhetoric
hours go by I play Ella
singing the same song ("when she
finished you could hear a rat piss
on cotton") and when Sinatra went
into short-lived retirement in 1971
that was his last song
'scuse me while I disappear
and the lights went out

This poem is a renewable
energy source every line
leads to the philosopher's
head-scratching ease among
conflicting ideas as he
taps the springs for empirical
evidence of the sudden
clarity though it lasts but
a few minutes like the time I
stood at the window of my room
in Cambridge eight years after
I had lived there and could see
what time had done to the bridge
and the lawns beside the river
in the Jesus Green nothing
had changed except the beholder but
the dimension of time stood out
among the ideas vying for eminence
in my mind as I looked tears came
to my eyes I turned to face
the stranger who lived there
now and that was sixteen years ago
and today's window looks out at
orange traffic posts and yellow cabs

Eighty-one degrees a record high for the day
which is not my birthday but will do until
the eleventh of June comes around and I know
what I want: a wide-brimmed Panama hat
with a tan hatband, a walk in the park
and to share a shower with the zaftig beauty
who lost her Bronx accent in Bronxville
and now wants me to give her back her virginity
so she slinks into my office and sits on the desk
and I, to describe her posture and pose,
will trade my Blake (the lineaments of a gratified
desire) for your Herrick (the liquefaction of
her clothes) though it isn't my birthday and
we're not still in college it's just a cup of coffee
and a joint the hottest thirtieth of March I've ever

# APRIL 2

I thought happiness wore a skirt
& two-inch heels on Eighth Street
that's when I was unhappy but now
it's Gerry Mulligan and "I Didn't
Know What Time It Was" on a day
when I feel like skipping breakfast
& strolling over to Lupa for lunch
and then what? I'll let the sun
surprise me and forget the high gusts
that made an awful racket last night
they were shooting a movie
on MacDougal Street yesterday
with Nicole Kidman someone said
and someone else said Ben Affleck
four giant trailers blocked off
the street now they're gone leaving
the sun beaming through
the windows that need washing
filtering the light that looks yellow
in the planetary currency exchange
the sun is gold and silver is the moon

# APRIL 3

It's one thing to rage
against decrepit old age
it's another thing to drink
yourself to death and I don't know
what made me think of Dylan
Thomas's farm forever fled
like a fleeting cloud only this one
dominates the sky on this chilly gray
afternoon Alfonso walks Piazza
singles to left and we have runners
on the corners with nobody out
the winning run on third base
and Zeile hits a fly ball to right
that will tie it up and it's still
cloudy and cool but better than being
in the office on opening day

The exodus from Egypt takes place
tonight this is the bread
of affliction this the wine
like the water of the Nile turned
into blood, the first plague
visited upon Pharaoh this is
the lamb of the feast the blood
of the lamb smeared on the doorposts
so the angel of death would know
which houses to pass over as he
came to slay the first-born sons
of the Egyptian ruling class these
are the bitter herbs fresh horse-
radish the sharpest most pungent
my mother served the tears
of many centuries and my father
poured the wine in Elijah's cup
that the prophet invisibly sipped
let all who are hungry join us

❦

## Savannah

One thing I can tell you
about the South: they still think
they should have won the war.
Yet on the corner of Liberty and Lincoln,
what's this I see? the American flag, and if I
walk a few blocks alongside magnolias
and leafy palms, I still believe it could be said
that more happened to me on that
forty-minute walk than to many men
in ten years, and I can see now that
change is the great subject for poetry
and therefore growing old (which,
as Ashbery said, "I never thought
I would do") is a matter of one's mind
keeping up (or going down) with one's body, and if
this were a novel it would say
the man with the old-fashioned leather briefcase
arrived in Savannah, birthplace of Johnny Mercer,
home of Flannery O'Connor (briefly). It was 8:30.
He deemed it wisest to dine alone
and make an early night of it.

The subway is a funeral
and I'm going down
to win Eurydice back
with my clarinet I don't
look back but when I
step into the light
I'm alone at Oren's Daily
Roast on Waverly Place
Richard Howard walks in
saying there are four areas
of human experience alien
to him they are baseball
jazz organ music and lace
what I like about this city
is you never know who
will show up to buy you
an espresso and console you
for the loss of the blonde
on the R train

I saw a sign saying
Religious Sex
so I walked in
& there was Melissa Rossi
who wrote a bio of
Courtney Love & I don't know
who she is & she doesn't know
who Wallace Stevens was
so we're even
there's something you don't know about me
like what?
like I like designing cigarette packs
Gemini cigarettes Leo cigarettes one for each
sign of the zodiac except Cancer
the young poet's a god
the old poet's a tramp
Joe's writing a book called
"Pardoning the Eye of the Beholder"
and the phone rings hello Dave
this is Charlie calling from hell

I asked Joe if you could save
one thing from a house on fire
what would it be? "The fire"
he said, which was the right
answer, not that I want to set
the world on fire I just want
to enter the nave of your heart
and leave a little flame in
the chapel as a parting gesture
today I feel your absence
most acutely like a clarinet
solo followed by a muted trumpet
and then the piano joins in
it's Red Norvo's All Star Quartet
with Irving Berlin's "Russian Lullaby"
in 1944 nice and easy what I see
is a bush in flames yet unconsumed
what I hear is a lazy melody

I may look dumb but I assure you I'm
one of the forty most powerful
men in this week's issue of New York,
New Work, New Yak, Not Yours,
No Yes, Nyet Yin, Nor Yang magazine
My self-image is Gregory Peck
in *Gentleman's Agreement* impersonating
a Jew as I impersonated a journalist
in my usual rush but with time enough
to cross the street where Joe's Pizza
opened to acclaim and a year later a
competing shop opened on the same
block, this one called Joe's Original Pizza
No, never you need Yonkers north Yoko
Net worth network in Newark
My new wok broke
Not with a yuk but a nuclear yoke

"I have something in common with
Franz Kafka," Franz Kafka wrote
in his journal but didn't say what.
He had agreed to cover the hooker olympics
in Las Vegas for a glossy magazine.
He marveled at his luck: he, a sickly young
boyo specializing in worker's compensation,
had been granted the opportunity to gamble
using the house's money. How could he lose?
But what he liked best about the myth was that
sooner or later he knew he would be
desperate to lose the Midas touch
like investors in a panic to dump their stocks
last Friday. As one stock jockey glumly noted,
"We need the greed line to exceed the fear line."
America spread out before him like a field
of goldenrod with aproned women stooping
to gather the fruit under the apple trees nearby.

Hitler was not born at Braunau-am-Inn in 1889
He did not become Germany's chancellor on January 30, 1933
which happens to be the birthday of Franklin D. Roosevelt
who was not inaugurated that March
The Weimar Republic did not fail
There was no ill-fated beer hall putsch in Munich in 1923
after which Hitler did not serve nine months in prison
during which he did not write *Mein Kampf*
World War I did not conclude with the humiliation
of the Germans at Versailles
nor were the windows of synagogues and Jewish shopkeepers
smashed in November 1938
Furthermore you (who are a pretty typical American)
have never heard of Hitler, Roosevelt, Weimar, or the Treaty
        of Versailles
for a very simple reason:
the only record of these people and events
is a novel that cannot be bought or sold
under penalty of death
This is my ode to Philip K. Dick

## Same Difference

It occurred to me
today that there's
no difference between
"thank you" and "fuck you"
so from now on
whenever someone says
"thank you" to you
think of it as "fuck you"
OK but what about
the next time someone
says fuck you to you
does that mean thank you?
No, I'm afraid it doesn't work that way
(he smirked)
That also means "fuck you"
all roads lead to the Rome of "fuck you"
get it?
I do but you don't have to be so
fucking in-my-face about it
Well, fuck you
No, fuck you

The universal language isn't music
it's sports or maybe it's English
as spoken on my block in New York
Harry who runs Silver Express next door
accepts UPS packages for me and
when I come in after a Knicks loss
he looks at me pained as if it were my fault
he's exulting now that we beat the Raptors
"but we still need a point guard"
while Nairobi native Abe who runs
the copy center up the block is
a Patrick skeptic who nevertheless likes
our chances against hated Miami
of course there is always an exception
in this case the Chinese laundry
of which I am also fond where
the radio transmits Chopin
and the lady from Shanghai
teaches me the words in Mandarin
Chinese (she knows no Cantonese)
for hello, thank you, no problem, and goodbye

Like an article in the newspaper
read in a moment of distraction,
in the subway or the john, and
forgotten right away, the memory
returned to me three days later
when you walked into the office
I'd know that scent anywhere
as a fly bothers a lightbulb
on a hot & hazy July morning
and the ceiling fan doesn't work
I followed you down alleys
in hollow lands and hilly lands
but who you were remained a mystery
no matter how much sex we had
in cheap bungalows in West Hollywood
when the sexiest thing I could think of
was a closet with nothing in it
except a woman's dress on a hanger
and it belonged to you

I'm quoting not repeating myself
there's a difference it's Cinco de Mayo
hot as June hot enough to sunbathe
nude on the roof twenty-three flights up
men in shirt sleeves or short sleeves
their pockets bulging with pens, combs,
sunglasses, wallet, keys, coins,
30% off coupons to Brooks Brothers,
eye women in the street & I'm one of the oglers
but it beats carrying a handbag
in Paris in 1977 I tried the vide poche
pocketbook for men nice black leather
but I kept losing it at the Rheims train station
in retrospect one of the happiest days
in my marriage that whole summer was
a honeymoon in France driving a Renault Douze
down the Loire then along the coast to Nice
then Vence in the Alpes-Maritimes
one day we drove to Italy for lunch
and many weeks and kilometers later
we drank a bottle of velvet bubbly
and spent the afternoon nude in bed
and that August day in Rheims
was as hot as today

*for Vincent Katz*

Joan Mitchell liked daylight
but also worked at night
in this sexy 1957 photo
by Rudy Burckhardt and
I love her huge abstract
"George Went Swimming
at Barnes Hole, but It Got
Too Cold" let's face it
your idea of the artist is
a jazz musician or abstract
painter forty years ago I
admit it I love black-and-white
photos of colorful painters,
Guston, Rothko, de Kooning,
fantasies in ebony pencil
with red and yellow crayons
and the word "faith" pronounced
in a Dutch accent "fate"

I watch TV for the plots
for example a corporate nun
accused of lesbianism is
convicted of killing the priest
who dumped her for a choir boy
while the CEO, an ex-racketeer,
has chronic impotence
and such an attractive wife
on the other hand I hate
it when a magazine show
plants cameras in the Aja bar
doing a story on men "who
won't commit" versus women
whose "biological clocks are
ticking" and my candidate for
the fake word of the year is
"edgy" as in "Anne Klein's edgy
statement" which consists of
tough boots and a chemise

*for Cynthia Todd Quam*

You can fly a hundred times
and you still get nervous waiting
at the airport for bad weather
in Chicago delaying all flights I'm
in a disaster movie called O'Hare
I recognize some of the actors
the dandy the guy who played Hamlet
in the Wall Street production
and Ophelia who did a nude scene
rain hail bolts of lightning a tornado
a flood and man it's cold I'm
dressed for Palm Springs, California,
and what am I doing in Chicago
I don't know but while I'm here
I may as well go
to Oak Park and visit Hemingway's
boyhood, and the wound

Ira Gershwin and I were talking
when George walked in smoking
a cigar I was surprised he was
alive I knew he had died young
but I was forbidden to reveal
this to Ira who showed me
his lyrics for "Someone to Watch
over Me" proud of the rhyme of "man
some" and "handsome" all three
of us wore white shirts and ties
and I remember thinking what a treat
to meet George Gershwin how
unexpected unlike meeting Ira
which is something I felt I had done
every day for years

The boy felt guilty
he had cursed god
for the suffering in the world
his father said
"don't feel guilty
god will forgive you
but what makes you think
you're as smart as god"
"I don't think I'm as smart as god"
"yet you judge him"
the father said irrefutably
the boy was quiet for a minute
"well even if he has his reasons
for the suffering in the world
I have my reasons too"
he said

In Rotterdam I'm
going to speak about
the state of poetry
on a panel with a Pole
and a Turk. It's worth
being alive to utter
that sentence. A
German from Fürth,
my father's hometown
and Henry Kissinger's,
will preside. His name
is Joachim Sartorius,
which sounds like a
pseudonym Kierkegaard
might use to condemn
the habits of his age
and ours when nothing
ever happens but the
publicity is immediate
and the town meeting
ends with the people
convinced they have
rebelled so now they
can go home quietly
having spent a most
pleasant evening

It fell on a Tuesday in 1940,
May 28, when Churchill told the cabinet
we shall fight it out, here or elsewhere
through disaster and through grief
to the ultimate defeat of our enemies
he won their hearts and a cheer went up
that was the turning point the moment
the British bulldog stood up to Hitler
who had miscalculated and it remains
an enigma why he spared the British army
at Dunkirk when he could have captured it
Churchill's speeches brought down
the house they made Labour members
cry they made Churchill cry too
they ended with a flourish like the mighty
Mississippi of history that keeps rolling
along let it roll let it roll on full flood,
on August 20, 1940
(and on the way back to 10 Downing Street
he sang "Old Man River" in the car)

What can you say about
the traffic in New York
some kid can shoot some
other kids in an Oregon
high school and it will cause
a forty-minute delay
on the FDR Drive
no use complaining
I'll get there just the same
in time to solve the Mansfield
murder the main clue
a pubic hair in the bathtub
So much happening so many
things that can go right and
all you need is one
and if anything goes wrong
I'll do what I always do
I'll leave I'll walk away no
I'll run away like the men
I imagined when I was a boy
leaving home with a stick
and small bundle of clothes
who stop at the newsstand
and buy the Hobo News
on their way to the subway

Eighty degrees isn't she lovely
a perfect day to take 13
to 281 to 81 North to the Syracuse
Jazz Festival in Clinton Square
where Nat King Cole's brother is
singing "Isn't She Lovely" you feel like
Benedict Arnold you say why I ask
because shouldn't we be at the Ithaca
Festival today no we shouldn't we should
be right here listening to the Freddy Cole
quartet with a couple of Billie Holiday
numbers including "Them There Eyes" a favorite
of mine I hope he sings the song
I heard on the radio last night
I'm speeding on coffee beer a cigarette
a kiss and the sun does it always flow
this easy you say no I answer
but my smile gives me away

I said OK Joe what makes
this flower beautiful
what makes the flower
a flower he answered
right again as we walked
down Valentine Place past
the students and the nursing
home down the cobblestone
street leading to the bridge
above Six Mile Creek where
myrtle grows wild I wonder
why Milton said "ye myrtles
brown" when they're green with
little purple buds in May

## Job Description

What I like about this place is
everyone has a job to do it's like
a war in that respect my job is
to get people to write things they
wouldn't otherwise have written
and to drop a phrase into their
dreaming minds at night your job
is to cross Sixth Avenue in a hurry
as the light changes that girl's job
is to eat a slice of Joe's pizza
her boyfriend's job is to wear
a Yankee cap and a Giuliani mask
hold on he *is* Giuliani and that guy
heckling him is a reporter whose
job is to remember Sirhan Sirhan who
shot Bobby Kennedy on this day
in 1968 a few minutes after I turned off
the television thinking he had just won
the California primary and would
be our next President

## THE LONELY CROWD

One of the amenities of hell is
the coffee break & you get to read on the subway
I'd forgotten how great *The Lonely Crowd* is
I was an inner-directed kid in an other-directed society
No wonder I became an oversexed drug addict
who vows never to forget you, Vietnam
In the free-fire zone let the word go forth
By the waters of the Hudson I mourned for you
The war was over over there but we were still fighting it here
That, too, changed everything along with sensitivity training
And the generals were still fighting the last war
expecting four years of trench warfare
instead of tanks overrunning France in five weeks

What is it about the Abyss
that tempts the young poet to kiss
the air and head for the nearest cliff? This
unreasonable attachment to the bliss
of falling—what accounts for it? Unlike the hiss
announcing a reptilian presence, the word *Abyss*
creates the object of our dread: it exists, it is,
widening like the gulf between whis-
key and wine, and we, drunk on neither, miss
the days when we, too, tumbled headlong out of heaven, pissed

There's a darker shade of blue
in the clouds dragging themselves
slowly across the lighter blue
of the sky: and the darkness
of green as the light leaves the trees,
the green of the pine and the green
of the yew alike leaking light
into the evening: a streetlamp
lets pedestrians and predators
pass or loiter in the languor
of a dark blue summer night,
but the darkness of the blue
is darker than the trees or
thoughts of blue men on porches
contemplating the blueness of the moon.

## IN THE HOSPITAL

In the hospital there was time
to read to dream to act
to read Freud's dream book on his couch
and how his best thoughts came to him
in the hospital during
World War I for example when
he invented a new way of opening
a vein while sitting in front of
a typewriter the wound
survived him but in the hospital
he knew only the words glory
and honor and country
rhymed with story
and malheur and the country
matters Hamlet lauded
in Ophelia's lap when mad
or pretending to be mad
and Denmark wasn't a prison
or brothel it was a hospital

∞

No man lived who had enough
of children's gratitude or women's love
so I have assembled you all here
for a little experiment let me begin
by introducing you please stand when
I call your name Mr. Fitzgerald to my
right is the ex-husband of the deceased
Mr. James over here is the father
of her children Mr. Crane where are you
ah there you are is the man who got away
and here is the man I will refer to as X
you will have exactly three days from
the time I finish speaking to figure out
which of you dispatched the bride you'll
do it if you want to get off this island
there's room for three in the rowboat

No better place to start the day
than the South End of Boston
the streets deserted and washed
by the ceaseless rain the tea party
in full swing in the living room
where books are planned a novel
called *Evenings with Stalin*
by Askold for example and now we
will go around the table and play
truth or dare the music provided
by Lester Young Sue says she loves
a song called "I Like Your Pants"
and hands me the CD in question
which turns out to be "Also Sprach
Zarathustra" and if I were Vincent
Youmans I'd give up my Schuberts and
Schumanns and concentrate on a high
romance with a girl in a black sweater
who gives me a chance to sidle up
to her and whisper "I like your pants"

I don't want a wall
separating the Language
poets from the New York
School but you say good
fences make good
neighbors that's because
at heart you're the last
American to believe
he stood at the center
of the universe just by
standing where he stood
on some peripheral perch
in the untamed wilderness
of winter you see no reason
to temper your scorn of us
weaklings hooked on the drug
of self you plant in spring
reap in August and are grim
as ever by November the wind
howling in the leafless branches
as you walk into the dark green
woods and a woodstack appears
across your path like a wall

The greatest genius in the history
of American marketing is the guy
who added the word "repeat"
to the directions on the back
of the shampoo bottle
you can spend a day like today
(too cool for a swim, too lazy to work)
watching the market as if it were
a ballgame with a late-inning Nasdaq
rally and we could rate fund managers
on their risk-adjusted, front-weighted
three-to-five-year average
relative to their benchmark index
but I feel like calling Glen, Gillian, Lloyd
& editing a volume of Henry James's
tales of writers and artists
I'm like the character in the hotel
of a poem by Guillaume Apollinaire
& the sun enters the room like an arm
whose hand holds a cigarette lighter
I don't want to work I want to smoke

We know who
the guards are
in those POW
movies with brutal
but easy to
fool fat Germans
or sadistic Japanese
who never smiled
they're the grown-ups
we're the kids
that's the secret

Gloomy day, chilly,
gray, yet still warm
enough to wear shorts
and read Agatha Christie
in the hammock as if
the last sixty years had
not taken place, the war
in Europe was about
to break, it was the last
summer of the dishonest
decade, tragic as Mahler's
Sixth Symphony, yet
time enough still for
one last detective novel
with the universally
despised victim in
the chamber locked
from within

### FOR ANNE

When I think of all the Annes
in my life they're all you almost
you're the Irish girl with the blonde
corkscrew curls in Cincinnati but
you're also Anne of the thousand
days and poems my mother's
name is Anne the heroine of my
novel of the twentieth century
which begins in Vienna moves
to London with Freud and sneaks into
New York during the "phony war"
in 1939 Anne is the name of the first girl
I loved and it's always spelled with an "e"
I lost my virginity to a Brandeis girl
named Anne and a Sarah Lawrence girl
named Anne lost hers to me I'm a big
fan of Anne and will always be

I looked at the moon
and couldn't find it
so I drove and refused
to ask for directions
I like getting lost
with you and how much
fun we had listening
to early Coltrane in
the morning the first
time we were nudes in
an anatomy textbook
with our body parts
identified in crude
English why should that
have charmed us so
wasn't it enough to
wake and know you were
there beside me though
day had intervened?
I can do anything,
I thought, and planned
to drive from New York
to Virginia stopping in
New Hampshire on the way

"Toys in the Attic" is a great title
for a movie or play that I never saw
in my attic I have a cigar box
full of buttons from the rhyming
fifties ("I Like Ike," "Madly
for Adlai") and militant sixties
("End the War Now: Local 1199,"
"Legalize Private Murder Why
Should the Government Have All
the Fun?") and one from college
with just the word "belly"
in red script on a white field
it was a forerunner of your
collection Joe so tell me
how's camp (happy birthday)

∞

I hate errors
the way Conrad's
Marlow in *Heart
of Darkness* hates
lies, which doesn't
stop him from
telling one, a
big one, to
Kurtz's girlfriend, whose
name was not
the last thing
said by Kurtz
unless her name
is "the horror!"
in which case
he says it
twice so I
apologize to you
for the typo
that turned "honey"
into "money" a
term of endearment
into filthy lucre

All my life I've lived
where Edgar Allan Poe lived
on the top floor
of the last cigarette I smoked
in the cockpit of the Spitfire
when the war ended
and it remained 1938
every knock on the door confirmed it
have you ever seen a hanging
well I have (I lied)
and it isn't a pretty sight
& now that I have everyone's attention
let me direct it to all
systems of belief founded on
the fear of anarchy
if I succeed I shall make men mad
women too
like a flower trapping a hapless insect
the desire to reproduce requires
a momentary union
& lifelong quarrel

# AUGUST 4

Days of ease and Keats's odes
"with beaded bubbles winking at the brim,"
full-throated mornings & warm afternoons
in the hammock on Valentine Place
and of course it helps that I'm in love
and listening to Art Blakey and the Jazz
Messengers, "Come Rain or Come Shine,"
another inspired Arlen and Mercer standard
in the jukebox of my mind, and you know what?
loving you, doll, has been all shine
just like this summer day and then
you call to report Rudy Burckhardt's
death in today's paper what a gentle
man he was with sad eyes, unfailingly
generous to me, and I love his photos
my favorite being a trompe l'oeil with
the Brooklyn Bridge in the artist's studio window
(someday I will use that on the cover of a book)
and he was 85, it was ruled a suicide, he drowned
in a pond in Searsmont, Maine, where his
beloved Edwin Denby ended his life
in 1983 well Rudy this is goodbye

I just got off the phone
with a prophet from
the Bronx who said
prayer is an obsessive-
compulsive formation you want
to have sex with everyone
you see but when you wake up
you want to pray you lie
in the dark afraid of the darkness
from which you have come and to which
you shall return until the dim
flickers of morning light let you
see that everything (yesterday's
clothes and books, the chair
you moved to replace the battery
in the defective smoke detector)
is just where it was last night

How did that bat get in here
last night & the weird thing
is that on August 13, 1993,
also a Friday, two bats flew
in here late at night Joe and
I chased one out and killed
the other with a broom we won't
forget we had dinner that night
with Alison Lurie in her garden
and just before midnight a waitress
called from California saying
her name was Marion Crane and
she was about to change from white
bra and white slip to black bra and
black slip & now she needs a shower

My new Web site is dropdead.com
It's interactive you get to choose how
you'll die, where, and at what age
and it'll still come as a complete
surprise to you I guarantee
but let's not get morbid it's a game
it's more fun than bullshit.com and a lot less
narcissistic than kissmyass.com
Michael Douglas will play the lead with Sandra
Bullock as a baby in an out-of-control
baby carriage going down the Odessa Steps
but that's just one scenario you can
create your own we're going to have an IPO
tomorrow you can buy shares at getrich.com

## Rap

I'm still here (Ithaca)
the students are back
they drive up next door
in a Mercedes sports car
the color of a school bus
hideous, with rap music
to announce their arrival they
leave the car running, the keys inside,
the music on while they go inside the house
I walk over remove the keys
toss them in the bushes walk away
unobserved & think of Ashbery's line
there's only one thing worse than rap music:
French rap music

The day still unwritten I wake
with a song that's how I know
I'm happy at ten o'clock
the furnace man cometh
and at ten thirty Jeremy who works
at Autumn Leaves is coming
to repair the fence the shower head
and the bookcase and teach me how
to disconnect the battery and
distributor in my car so it can spend
the winter in my Ithaca garage Jeremy
is like my acupuncturist they both
think they can cure anything
now Judith Moore is on the phone
dishing dirt too hot for this poem
and now Charles Simic is back
in Yugoslavia remembering how
he and his little pals, like the kids
in *Carmen,* played soldiers:
"The war went on, bombs fell,
and we played soldiers"

I took off my watch
and saw the skin beneath
the dog it was past one
o'clock and Mayakovsky's
suicide note was in his
pocket a poem praising
all creation in speechless
wonder I lived my life
through without a clock
expecting failure as in
a "modern" novel, you
know the surveyor will
never reach the castle,
the coward proves valorous
but dies in the attempt,
we can't really believe in
happiness and in success,
Borges concluded, and that is
why Kafka wanted his books
burned he had wanted to write
a happy book but it would have
been a lie and his job was
to tell the truth not the truth
of facts but the truth of his dreams

## COMMENCEMENT

They're calling old people seniors
short for senior citizens but it's as though
they're still in college and can look forward
to graduate school at Purgatory State
or the University of the Damned and
I can see this poem is intent on being Catholic
though it started out agnostic
Maybe that's because I was talking
to Ed Webster on the phone tonight
and he described himself as an agnostic
who got a job teaching at a Catholic school
in the South Bronx or maybe because I was reading
the classifieds in the *Daily News* today
and several greeted dead ones in heaven
in any case I like seniors maybe the rest of us
are juniors and sophomores and we still have
the junior prom and all that romantic angst
to go through before we reach the holy land

The last Campbell's tomato soup can
of the twentieth century is going to
the Andy Warhol Museum in Pittsburgh
That is an example of a sentence
Another is this from a CEO in *Fortune*
"You die in either case, but this way you get
to do it proactively," where the adverb
makes the sentence I'm walking amid
the tourists on Bleecker Street the riffraff
the students with backpacks the bums and
a good old-fashioned New York feeling
hits me from head to toe a misanthropic snarl
the urge to kick a stranger in the pants,
and if you don't smoke you feel as if you do

When he threw the roach
out the window of the car
returning to the city from
the island M. got mad
at him and he wondered
whether it was because
(1) M. was against litter
(2) M. thought the act
might attract the interest
of a cop (3) M. felt that
the roach was the best
part of a joint, or (4) M.
was angry by disposition
well it was nice to be
in the passenger seat
of a car driving into
the filthy city air
on a night without traffic
when all the lights are green
sometimes you can hear
the city groaning

## Happy Anniversary

You've been together
thirty-nine months
do I think that's
significant I do why
thirty-nine is the number
of months you need to be
accident-free to erase
traffic violations from
your driving record it's
the number of lines
in a sestina the number
of "Steps" in Hitchcock's
dream of espionage with
the male and female leads
handcuffed together
overnight on the train
to the distant north

# SEPTEMBER 1

Dr. Schlissel, high Austrian
official, pulled me aside
and said he would tell me
the meaning of this joke
what joke, I said
any joke, he answered
and that's why I have come
to Vienna to visit the hostel
for homeless men where
a failed architect ate soup
and plotted my grandparents' death
to Vienna
I have come to listen
to the Waldmeister Overture
while my mother, confused,
speaks German to me
and English to the Viennese

There's a disease that
eats away at English.
It's called Anger Management.
Let me teach you.
You go to a singles' bar
on Sixth Avenue where the noise
would be described as "deafening"
if I were a journalist
and you were European, Danish or Dutch,
planning to get into a fistfight
with a German just to see
whether I, the American, will intervene
to break it up, but I'm not going
to play that game I'm a New Yorker
I refuse to get involved.

Sprewell is the Marlon Brando
of the Knicks and the definition
of Schadenfreude is my hollow laugh
when I tell you how Frank Kermode
lost two-thirds of his library
to the men he thought were movers
who were actually garbagemen
and the one-third of his library
spared was literary theory
which he used to be tolerant of
in a laissez-faire spirit but
has grown to detest now that
it no longer matters what
he thinks and you say Columbia
paid him not to teach the way
the government pays farmers not
to farm their land and now I know
how I want to spend this lazy day
the Sunday of Labor Day weekend
in my pajamas with a pot of coffee
all morning and you on the phone

Not a day without a notation
each woman loved because of
a woman she reminded me of
is that true no it's a theory
I'm going to kiss those lying lips
of yours for oh love's bow
shoots buck and doe and the impulse
to theorize is irresistible in
the evening sun we came as close
to having sex as two people could
without having sex in the nude swimming
capital of upstate New York & though
I've never seen her since I feel about
that girl as did Everett Sloan about
the girl he saw on the ferry
in his memory when he was suffering
from old age, the disease whose cure
is worse than the ailment, in *Citizen Kane*

# SEPTEMBER 8

In summer camps
in Hancock and Port Jervis
East Greenbush and Red Hook
when my father sent me week-old
box scores from the *Times*
so I could see how Koufax
and Drysdale were doing,
I wondered what it felt like
to wear a shirt and tie
on a muggy New York afternoon
sweating in my shirt and
letting the sweat on my forehead
cool on a day of high volatility,
low volume and not much change
in the averages: and now I know

See this picture and I guarantee
you won't drive your car into one
of those automatic car washes
where you put your car in neutral
and it moves along the rails,
brushes and hoses attack,
and hit men handcuff the doors
and prepare to torture you as in
a dream already over and you
remember it without commercial
interruption two hours of nonstop
violence condensed into two
minutes of terror though that's not
how the night began it began
with drugs, kinky sex, Burroughs
talking to himself ("I had a habit:
it kept me occupied") and Mario
Savio in Berkeley in 1964 saying
there comes a moment when
the operation of the machine
makes you so sick at heart
you can't take part

And this promise I thee make
if pain or grief be thy portion
I shall visit you, my dream
with Tommy Dorsey's girl
singers singing "On the Sunny
Side of the Street" and when
you open the door I shall
impersonate Hurricane Floyd
and you can be the South
Carolina coast you won't need
to watch it on TV it's a Thursday
but it feels like a Friday like a
short afternoon in November
dark wet windy we've received
a foot of rain, and a foot of rain
is what my shoe feels like so
let's cook meat loaf
for dinner plus Ida Lupino's
*The Hitchhiker* what say

Thanks to the hurricane
I had a waterfall out
the bathroom window
and a pond below
which evaporated
overnight like a poet's
reputation or a day
trader's profits and
the huge broken branch
of the ash tree finally
fell to the ground
the rain was an orchestra
with trombones, trumpets
and a great percussion
section now gone though
I've still got Sonny Stitt
playing "I've Got Rhythm"

Everything means something
as the "countdown to the unknown"
(Alan Greenspan's phrase) continues
for example tonight's the fight
between Felix Trinidad and Oscar de la Hoya
and we're driving to the republic of Flushing
with Stacey up front and a black star in the back seat
to watch it with our host the poet Frank Lima
who was an assistant chef at the Kennedy White House
and will serve longevity noodles on paper plates
you make a left at Dunkin' Donuts on 147th Street
then a right on 35th Avenue and you're there
I hear Bob Holman is coming will he bring Elizabeth Murray
I wonder so why don't I phone him and find out
it's ringing he answers "poetry" I say "this is prose"
and we resolve to duke it out on pay-per-view tonight
yes she is coming I just saw her cover for a book of poems
by Lee Ann Brown called *Polyverse* and want to see more
and I will bring this poem and ask everyone if it's true

## Jam Today

It's too late to sell too soon to buy
That's the Street's way of saying
jam yesterday and jam tomorrow but never
jam today I remember when Tom Disch
was going to start a literary magazine called
"Jam Today" I wonder what happened to that idea
today I heard the phrase "let's get freaky,"
yesterday "drama queen" entered my New York
apartment and transformed it by her very presence
in the dimmed light and tomorrow Alex Duran
will note that "bitchslap" has made it into the OED,
sooner or later I guess we're all
like the Russian émigrés in a Nabokov story
understood by no one but ourselves
did he say "earnings" no he said "warnings"
and I dig your opal earrings
do I exit no I exist
& I don't want to be late
for tonight's jam session
with Eric Alexander on tenor sax

### Shuttlecock

"I'm a workaholic,"
he confided. That was
the down side of sitting
at the bar at seven p.m.
People kept talking
to the unpaid listener
who pronounced *Grand
Marnier* "grand mariner"
as in Prageeta Sharma's
poem that she read
at KGB last night plus
her "Ode to Badminton"
which was the upside
of being at the bar at eight

In two weeks it will be thirty-three years
since the fire in Alfred Leslie's life
and nearly sixty years since
his first wife's cousin was Pirandello's
secretary, was he hard-of-hearing then too
yes but he discovered he could read lips one day
in the park when from fifty feet he heard
what the governess said to the boy he can
watch TV without the sound lucky man
who can see what he needs to hear
cut up and splice is his method
and when he makes a photo-silkscreen
print of a movie still of Richard Conte
chasing a murderer down a hill
in 1947 it's as if he had taken the photo
himself and saved it from the fire

If I'm invisible it's inevitable
but so is Johnny Hartman's voice
and John Coltrane's sax
which makes me think of sex
as something finer than the grapefruit
Jimmy Cagney of Stuyvesant High School
pushed into the face of his movie wife
one reason for dining at Le Gigot is
no one will push a grapefruit in your face
another is the waiter's excellent taste
in music & I'm wearing
sunglasses to hide bloodshot eyes
I woke up alone, with cuts on my neck
and scratches on my forehead
who knows what battles I fought
in my sleep and did I win well I survived

While I wondered about the relation
of fraud to Freud and both to joy
my Wellesley girlfriend, a dyslexic
classics major, wanted to discuss
the "myth of syphilis" meanwhile
Jim Cummins confesses he lives in
"a witness protection program called
Ohio" and the critics sit in judgment
of John Keats and what he meant
by melancholy in his ode "I think
Keats is saying 'deal with it' " one says
not the one who calls him John Maynard
Keats but you can't have everything
("bucks, tenure") all you can count on
is unremitting indifference
broken up by patches of hostility

## London Fog

To the novelist, the fog itself
sets the scene: an adulterous affair
in wartime London and he is a sinner
and she becomes a saint you have it all
sex sin and unlimited guilt an exquisite
punishment for a harmless vice and in
this scenario there has to be a boy corrupted
by what he sees he, too, has his vices
he is a Yeshiva boy in postwar New York
and it's the ten days between Rosh Ha'shanah
and Yom Kippur when God weighs all in
the balance so what does he do he steals
some nickel-and-dime items he doesn't need
from Woolworth's and has sex with a stranger
in a raincoat the guilt was unbearable but he
bore it as Samuel's mother bore her anguish

Did you see the debate
between Bore and Gush
last night while the Yanks
got beat and did you notice
neither of them made any
reference to Hamlet who
(Empson said) kept his secret
by telling everyone he had one
these guys I feel I know
from college one belonged to
the gin-and-juice fraternity
the other wore a blue blazer
and was captain of the debate
team arguing for and against
disarmament he's the smart guy
I was a smart guy once myself
but never felt I was being educated
until Columbia which was the height
of my ambition a great place
until my friends and I got there

Capitalism rules
you can own 100 shares
of MCI-Worldcom & happily
make money though you'd never
let MCI handle your phone
service is that an example
of holding contradictory ideas
in the mind at the same time
& continuing to function, which
Scott Fitzgerald said was the test
of a first-rate intellect and
is quoted almost as much
as his "no second acts in
American life" completely untrue
look at Nixon and nameless others
foot fetishists who become newspaper
columnists, plagiarists who become
TV producers, capitalism is
the mother who forgives all her sons

## STUMP SPEECH

And if I am elected
I shall become
Walt Whitman and see
the manure and smell
the white roses and prefer
the aroma of my armpits
finer than prayer
I shall defeat death
not the old-fashioned way
with religion or art
but on the wings
of an extraordinary liberty
I shall visit the past
and future from my restless
perch in the unsatisfied
moment that I shall never
arrest I solemnly swear

It's a great day for New York
thanks to Todd Pratt of the Mets
whose tenth inning homer beat Arizona
so now the Mets will face Atlanta
for the pennant and Joe and I yelled
as loud in the living room as if we were
at Shea and that's not all there was
a killer play at home plate it's a cool
sixty-three degrees I've got a great view
of the harbor birds lights small craft
a Cunard cruise ship the statue with
Emma Lazarus's lines the green top
of the Woolworth building the sun
imitating a Monet at the Met I feel
like breaking into a trot but Joe
says it's too serene to run

Guess whose birthday it is
hint: his first name rhymes with felonious
and Keats wrote that
the imagination was his monastery
and he was its monk
I'll have that scotch straight, no chaser
and Joe will have his Pepsi with a twist
and Pepsi is the name of Emma McCagg's dog
where Joe and I are posing for a double portrait
this rainy afternoon of quietness
with Milt Jackson dead at 72
I may be too old to be a bohemian
but he was too young to die

The language is full of sad words
but the saddest of these is Dad
the contest between fathers and sons
is an unequal one like the proportion
of combat to uneasy non-aggression
in *War and Peace* or World War II
still the weekend has to be counted
a success with two meals cooked by Dad
duck in Chinatown last night and a bacon-
burger for breakfast this morning at Aggie's
the Mets won, *The Blair Witch Project*
was spooky as advertised and there were
surprises too I think I like those the most
and now for a serene (his word) moment
in Joe's honor in Washington Square Park
awful noise of boom boxes I don't hear them
the sky like a body of water blue
with a single sail and light wind

When I called Latrell Sprewell
the Marlon Brando of the Knicks
I don't know what I meant but today
Mike Piazza stands in relation to the Mets
as Brando does to *The Godfather* he's the key
even when he isn't there (part 2 or game 4)
I'm glad I cleared that up
and while I'm at it may I point out
that the Modern Jazz Quartet rehearsed
four hours a day, three days a week
and Dizzy's band when they played at the Spotlight
the saxophones rehearsed for hours the reed section for hours
and they were incredible that night so spontaneous
thus does improvisation require careful preparation
in the choreography of basketball as in jazz

Trippers and askers surround me
Not one of them capable of lying
Nothing, in brief, but maudlin confession
"Now I can marry the girl"
An admirable woman and a frightful disaster.
They kill us for their sport.
I run to death, and death meets me as fast,
But we shall here remain because this place is a haven
Whom thus the Angel interrupted mild
With beaded bubbles winking at the brim:
This is where the serpent lives, the bodiless,
If what we could were what we would.
Why is a pale white not paler than blue?
The clown came out to inform the public
Who thought it was a jest and clapped
The earth not earth but stone and sun.
But stories somehow lengthen when begun.

Today I am going to write blurbs
that take risks
& shine like smooth pebbles in the sun
"A joint." "Major."
"Stalin would have shot the author."
"These poems are worth more
than 100 shares of Microsoft."
"I would be willing to go to jail
if that meant the author could
live another year." "If they execute me
these are the poems I want on my lips."
"Honest, courageous, no bullshit."
"Burns with a hard gem-like flame."
"Cool. He should have gone into politics."
"Reminds us that exuberance is delight."
"She knows men." "She knows me."
"A voice like no other." "Grabs you
by the throat." "By the short hairs."
"Better than Prozac." "Deeply felt."

Byron was right
the true Don Juan
is not an Italian tenor
sentenced to damnation
not a melancholy
commitment-phobic
philosopher in Copenhagen
but a passive
good-natured
good-looking
young fellow prone
to seasickness who
lets the girls
make the first move

What can you say about the Mets
down three games to none
one run down with six outs to go
Cedeno singles steals second Mora walks
they pull off a double steal
and Olerud singles them home
off the previously unhittable John Rocker
(look at his eyes, he's so intense
he looks cross-eyed) and we're still alive
and I'm still fourteen years old
and the kids in the movie about summer camp
are beatniks and this is the 1960s
the early 1960s of Maury Wills
on the basepaths and Ray Charles
on the radio and chemistry biology
geometry locker-room cruelty and daily masturbation
what a relief to return to 1999
in time for Benitez to strike out
the Braves' last batter

Can a woman be
a phallic symbol?
My English teacher says
the Statue of Liberty
is a phallic symbol
but I don't think so
I had an English teacher
like that once really what
was he like he was a she
and she said Death
Death and she were like
two old friends spending
quality time together
My thesis is that Emily
Dickinson was dead when she
wrote her poems that's how
she knew death was a driver
and a gentleman

This is the chess of baseball
we pull Wendell they pull Lockhart
then Professor Hershiser comes on
and retires the side on five pitches
and Melvin Mora, the Marcus Camby
of the Mets, throws a perfect strike
to nail Ryan Klesko at third base
and still the season ends cruelly
last night though technically already today
a today filled with the need
to pack for Los Angeles rent a car
change hotels and collude with Amy Gerstler
pausing for a minute or two
to write this poem in favor of the Mets
and the pleasure they gave us wait till next year

## L.A. CONFIDENTIAL

Auden called Rilke
the Santa Claus of
loneliness now how
can you top that you
can't but you *can* go
to Carol Muske's party
and imbibe bubbly at the bar
Hi I'm Heather from USC
Hi I'm David from the USA
and there's Leo Braudy
who has my birthday and
Molly Bendall who has a new
book and the same initials
as Melissa Berton and Stephen
Yenser says only the suits wear
suits in LA and David St. John
and Amy Gerstler and Benjamin
Weissman and Bernard Cooper
and I are all writing books
about you, Kenneth Koch,
also present it's April Fool's
Day in my heart and Dorothy
Braudy's painting is on
the wall and hello to you
Mark Doty Fred Dewey
Leslie Slote and Ralph Angel
how did Larbaud put it
"and I, being all those people
myself, who am yet
only a baboon"

That year I had no car radio
I didn't need one
I had a very entertaining mind
& could only afford a 1971 Impala with a hole in its oil pan
and this was 1981 with a wood stove in Ludlowville
a hot July rainy August chilly September dank November
with the four dogs, Bruno, Kelly, Bucky, & Gordon, & no dough
the woods near my house enchanted me with their chuckling
brooks and falls, hidden paths & no one to explore them
but me the noise of the wood burning in the stove at night
equaled the noise of the falls in the afternoon
but little thought what wealth the show to me had brought
that lonely morning not foreseeing the limited future
that companionless day with no vision of tomorrow

This is the music
that makes me happy
makes you want to
dance makes us feel
like the aristocrats
of jazz the Duke and
Duchess swinging
as "Don't Get
Around Much
Anymore" is played
by David "Fathead"
Newman who got
the nickname because
he couldn't read
the music he had to
memorize it and
the nickname stuck
except for Ray Charles
who called him "Brains"

After much deliberation
I have made up my mind
Life may be painful, sad,
charming, amusing, unkind
the one thing it cannot be
is boring that is why I've
assigned Mozart to a certain
great jazz clarinetist and
allowed myself the luxury
of not having to make a choice
at the museum I can have
my Matisse and Picasso too
my Pollock and de Kooning
though academics claim you
can have only one or the other
that's why they're academics
and write letters denouncing
their ex-friends in journals
edited by people who can't write
for people who won't read

Are you pissed off
yes I am I don't know why
maybe it's because the clocks
went back an hour last night
bringing darkness at five o'clock
and the Halloween parade
at six it's nice to know Joe
will sport trench coat and floppy
hat and magnifying glass and
a phony French accent conducting
his little friends Liam and Austin
in Ithaca tonight I think his best
costume ever was probably
the papier-mâché Big Ben still
in my garage upstate while I
play Monk and maybe Sinatra
whose records chart the manic
and depressive sides of my
personality with equal tact

There are several ways of looking
at the veteran timewaster
who asked me to lunch today
and stuck me with the tab
He's an insomniac a husband
who catches another man
looking lasciviously at
his wife's ass he's an
ass man himself he sells
insurance but used to be
the guy who sold me my
first computer and before that
was elected class president
in high school now lives in
Westchester smooth as ever
and when he shaves some mornings
the guy in the mirror is a dead
ringer for Clinton

You know what
the greatest sound
in the world is?
It's the sound of
a cellophane
candy wrapper
in the row
behind you
during Elizabeth
Frank's "attention
must be paid"
speech in *Death
of a Salesman*
makes me love
my fellow man
a little more
each time

You meet this pathetic guy
even his wife knows he's a loser
you feel sorry for him and befriend him
you go to a ballgame maybe or a museum
he's not such a bad guy maybe a little loud
a bit of a braggart who likes to argue
at least he has strong convictions
not necessarily you hear him argue
the opposite of what he argued last week
you see him at parties six months go by
you feel about him as everyone else does
but you were open-minded about it
and are not relying on reputation
but on your own experience
in forming the judgment that he's a jerk

"The House of Dr. Edwards"
is where I lived when I lived
with all the other refugees
who loved America in my
dreams of the 21 Club in New York
where the amnesiac imposter
plays poker with blank cards
and Ingrid Bergman's father
is Sigmund Freud in Rochester
and after that ordeal I'll
join Michael O'Hara and Mrs.
Arthur Bannister in court
where the defense attorney on
crutches cross-examines himself
and the cast of the yacht
reconvenes in the hall of
mirrors she didn't know how
to shoot a gun she said he said
you just pull the trigger

In college the first theme
you had to write
was on the American dream
and the evil of all materialism
except dialectical materialism
what reminded me of that?
the nine fifty I paid to see
this worthless movie in
the theater where in 1966
the two men pretended
not to know each other
but I saw the white man give
the black man a briefcase
I wondered what was inside
maybe a manuscript that told
the truth about Soviet Russia
if they could smuggle it
into the United States
he would live the American dream

I keep thinking of Apollinaire
whose poems I don't have with me
so I'll have to trust my memory
of "Zone" where he walks around
Paris the posters are prose poems
the bridges along the Seine are sheep
the Eiffel Tower a shepherdess
the refugees at the Gare St. Lazare
dream of making l'argent in the Argentine
and there are exotic birds and "you,
Pope Pius IX, only you are modern
among the Europeans," with Jesus
an aviator and the windows following
the poet from street to street until
the sun comes down or is guillotined

## A Quick One Before I Go

There comes a time in every man's life
when he thinks: I have never had a single
original thought in my life
including this one & therefore I shall
eliminate all ideas from my poems
which shall consist of cats, rice, rain
baseball cards, fire escapes, hanging plants
red brick houses where I shall give up booze
and organized religion even if it means
despair is a logical possibility that can't
be disproved I shall concentrate on the five
senses and what they half perceive and half
create, the green street signs with white
letters on them the body next to mine
asleep while I think these thoughts
that I want to eliminate like nostalgia
O was there ever a man who felt as I do
like a pronoun out of step with all the other
floating signifiers no things but in words
an orange T-shirt a lime green awning

Like Sinatra the day his voice cracked on stage
is how I feel today as if I had punched a stooge
at nineteen minutes before five there's no hope
for modernism nothing can stop the hype
no reason for the sheep in the dining room
or the diners unable to leave days pass the cream
rises to the top you make me want to be bad
come on forget your troubles be happy in bed
with me there's a new magazine on the net
called "Failure" I tried to access it today but could not
aha I got the Zen of the experience you say a hail Mary
& the Prime Minister of Japan is named Memento Mori
the subway map is an embryo with a green heart
some call it poetry but I know how much it hurt

You want to know what war is?
I'll tell you what it is
It's Pepsi versus Coke
for control of Venezuela
It's Pfizer versus American Home Products
for Warner Lambert's drug pipeline
a hostile takeover a poison pill a proxy fight
It's what they mean when people say
they "mean business" yet these companies
are also like baseball teams
the Microsoft Yankees the Intel Dodgers
they'll fight you in the ballparks
in the court rooms in the board rooms
and issue trading cards collect all 500

∽

It's Johnny Mercer's birthday
from Natchez to Mobile
in the cool cool cool of the evening
very cool with Barbara Lee
singing Marian McPartland playing
the greatest revenge songs of all time
hooray and hallelujah
you had it comin' to ya
and a bottle of Rodenbach
Alexander red ale from Belgium
with cherries and "Tangerine" in
the background in *Double Indemnity*
he had a feel for the lingo, "Jeepers Creepers"
as Bing Crosby sang it on my birthday
in 1956 I just played it three straight times
and an all-American sense of humor what does
Jonah say in the belly of the whale he says man
we better accentuate the positive that's it
happy birthday and thanks for the cheer
I hope you didn't mind my bending your ear

Being an evil man
I'll burn you like a candle
and I'll burn you on both ends
that's my blues for the day, and
forget tomorrow
as Frank wrote, the past is a
future that came through
that's my haiku
of the day and here's to you
Charles Bukowski
the comment on your last book
of poetry you liked best was
"you jack-off motherfuck,
you're not fooling anybody,"
my motto of the day

Poetry is
posing a
question to
the universe
and getting
no for
an answer
or getting
no answer
I'm not
sure which

According to Willa Cather
whose novel
*The Professor's House*
I'm reading
the place to place
a DON'T KNOCK sign
is on your desk
not on your door
puzzling your visitors
who "never get wise"
there's a lesson there but
don't make me explain it
please I want the luxury
of pathos (not pity)
the professor won't vacate
the cramped quarters of
his attic study for a spacious
modern new office here he is
on the cusp of becoming
an old man and dying

What a night what a light what a moon
white with patches of blue snow & here I am
striding longlegged to the bar on East 4th Street
Never was a Martini more deserved
The hot water pipe in my apartment sprang a leak
soaking a couple dozen books, magazines, files
There is renewed evidence of mice
My left eye has begun to twitch
after two and a half hours on the Taconic
and then to play War & Chicken on New York streets
but I had Mingus and "Fables of Faubus"
to keep me awake while you slept
and now the city, which suspended its activity
in my absence, has come back to me
with exciting new crises a haystack of mail
and thee O silver moon

the one thing that could
and the woman with the husky
never tires of being told
to bare one shoulder
of America I hear the phone
"I got old"
as Michael Gizzi wrote
"a wasp is a dead flower with wings"
and her last words were
ringing and the textbooks shut
voice has arranged her sweater
with the goddesses in an uproar
lipstick, shadow, what may
never happen to me happened

In the hothouse atmosphere
of Fairchild Gardens
the branches of exotic trees have
intercourse in the open
but at a speed too slow for
the human eye to detect so
let's listen to a Cuban rhapsody
let's drive down 95
avoiding the mound of garbage
that so inspired Archie and
then let's gossip about
the three Steins (Einstein,
Wittgenstein, and Gertrude Stein)
versus the four Bergs (Harold
Rosenberg, Clement Greenberg,
Moe Berg, and Alban Berg) in a
philosophy slam where each team has
to act out Hegel's position
on history without using words

# DECEMBER 4

When the sun sets in San Francisco
it's dark all over the world
that's what I mean by the evening sun
you pick up your pen
a piece of paper materializes
my mother tells her story
of crossing the Atlantic in a storm
in the last crossing the President Harding made
with her affidavits in order
seasick all the way, the last Thursday
in November 1939 it was, and for me it was
the first time, Thanksgiving dinner
when my time comes I want to drop dead
no homes for me no nurses no doctors
to be gone in an instant with no pain
in a lifetime without many wishes granted
is that too much to ask

There are days I wake up without waking up
in my robe or yesterday's clothes unshaven
I sit at the computer with the jazz station on
my Bose Wave radio, birthday present to myself
last June, and it's past one forty in the afternoon,
months have gone by and a shower sounds good
right now but the poem I'm writing is better
because of Ray Charles and Betty Carter, "Baby,
It's Cold Outside," and then "Beans and Cornbread
Had a Fight" with Rhonda Hamilton as referee on
Dave Brubeck's 80th birthday & I have
an amazing amount of work to do but that's how
these poems get written, as a holiday from all else
I'm supposed to be doing
just as prose is a holiday from the rigors of verse
in Shakespeare's plays *Hamlet* for example what
a piece of work is a man how noble in reason how

As I sit at my desk wishing
I did not have to edit a book
on poetry and painting a
subject that fascinates me
usually, but today is not as
usual, being today, white sky,
decent amount of sunlight,
forty one degrees in Central Park,
and it makes sense to dream of
next week in Chicago, another city
with two major league ballclubs,
and the pleasure of seeing Paul
and you, too, Elaine, whom
I never get to see often enough
in our own city of the Subway Series
champagne at the gallery and
the tech wreck on Wall Street,
and as I look out the window
almost any minute I expect
the brokers to fall from the sky
like Icarus in Brueghel's painting in
Auden's "Musée des Beaux Arts"
(and so back to work)

Fathers die twice
a year in Judaism
my father died today
twenty-eight years ago
in the secular calendar
and on 20 Kislev (November
29 this year) in the Hebrew
so I mourn on both dates
with a candle after many
ghostly reappearances
in Elsinore my home for
all the big speeches and
years I thought Freud's
Hamlet was the true one and
could be played by me in my
daily life while at night I moon-
lighted as Samuel Taylor Coleridge

He was in favor of
anything that gets you
through the night,
tomorrow night,
the longest night
of the year with
the brightest full moon
in one hundred
and thirty something
years. It called for
a celebration. He
felt like James Cagney
in the glory of being
killed at the end of *White Heat:*
"Made it, Ma. Top of the world!"

What Delmore Schwartz meant by
the beautiful American word "Sure"
is what I think not only in the movies
where dead men walk and change
identities with the men they killed
but in brokerage offices where grandmas
sell their bond funds to buy something
with dot-com in its name no wonder I'm in
my perennial hurry walking so fast
with only sugar and coffee to speed me
along yes speed is the subject
of the painting as Schuyler said of Kline
in the crossword puzzles of light and shadow
beneath the elevated tracks of the 1950s

The question what
was worth saving
the answer everything
nothing it means the
same thing look at
these two photos
and see what life has
done to this little boy
all aboard the twentieth
century limited with
three hoboes left behind
I believe they should give
book awards ten years
after the fact and negative
awards for books
overvalued when new
that's my idea of the day
now I'm off to Barbara's
annual party the best

Deny loss.
Discriminate the Lawrences (DH, TE).
Dominate the landscape.
Deliver legs defeat legends.
Love drama. Lament diaspora. Lave, dove.
London days. Let Debussy declare delight.
Look dreamy like a displaced lepidopterist.
Languid, droll. Or drastic, loose.
Ladykillers, do link dolls do.
Libertines deliver the libido, late date.
Don't lie lowdown deep;
declassify the light, and the lift-gate, deflate.
A lifelong diary delves debonair likeness.
Last dance. Let die the literary debate.
Delectable ludic Dioscuri lumpen-proletariat.
Lullaby Dulcinea during lookout. Dub louche.
Live dungarees. Dangerous, long. Drive left. Drift lucky.
Drink, lover. Learn double. Doubt louts. Decry lobbyists.
Don't let 'em lemon the doodad library.

## ODE TO JOURNALISM

I love journalism
because you get to use
phrases like "moral calculus"
in book reviews
It's always the end of an era
starring Lionel Trilling our Jew
in a leather jacket and unfiltered
Camels the liberal elite think tank
chic hangout mental watusi take it to the bank,
a neo-jerk no-brainer. As Mary Warner
to Louis Armstrong, who kissed her
lips as fervently as his trumpet, so you,
O journalism, are to me though I am wise
to your ways I must admit it's true
I'm as implicated in you as was the sailor
in the havoc wreaked by his pet orangutan
in Poe's "Murders in the Rue Morgue" you can
say what you like about journalists they're not bad guys.
It's critics I despise.

## QUINE'S END

When they quizzed Quine on the existence of physical objects
yes he said in practice as a matter of convenience
but there was no epistemological distinction between Homer's gods
and the furniture in the living room no distinction
between contingent truths (the train doesn't stop here anymore)
and definitive ones (all men must die) born in 1908
majored in math at Oberlin, in Europe he met
the logical positivists, returned to Harvard,
said, "an explanation—not the deepest one, but of a shallower kind—
is possible at the purest behavioral level" that was
the century's philosophy for you logical pure and shallow
had the question mark removed from his typewriter
in the Navy in World War II decoded German
submarine cipher first marriage second marriage
"I am deeply moved by occasional passages
of poetry, and so, characteristically, I read
little of it," collected stamps, liked to cross borders,
had a talent for drawing portraits and maps

There are two scenarios
in one the market crashes
our hero loses some money
not all being a conservative
sort with a wife whose
charms were wasted on him
in the other the market crashes
and he loses most of his money
and goes off to fight the Trojan
War in either case there's
only one constant and that's
Heisenberg's Uncertainty
Principle the old reliable it hadn't
failed him yet though everything
else was changing well it was better
after all to be the author of the epic
than any of the characters even
the heroes Hector saying goodbye
to Andromache holding their baby

Tonight's the night, as Woody Allen said of death
"I just don't want to be there at the time"
having lived through *War and Peace* would one
be more likely or less likely to look out the window
and not see the Russian Revolution a red blazing ball
I never thought I'd see the Berlin Wall
collapse and end the history of the spy novel
but that, too, has happened the century ended
eight years ago a short century with three major global
wars (two hot, one cold) some days you feel
you live in a museum but this isn't one of them
this is a day for reading Wallace Stevens aloud
"The Bird with the Coppery, Keen Claws" and
think of what a work associate said of Mr. Stevens
"Well, if you leave out his personal life, he was
a happy man" Joe is disappointed
that he can't visit his cousins in New Jersey
but we won't let our disappointment show or turn
to bitterness the disease of artists we just want
to look out the window and see the clouds
change shape and go in their direction

Grateful acknowledgment is made of the publications, print and electronic, where poems from *The Evening Sun* first appeared, in several cases with titles instead of (or in addition to) dates. These include *The American Enterprise, Antioch Review, Barrow Street, Bellevue Literary Review, Boston Review, Boulevard, Can We Have Our Ball Back?, Connecticut Review, Crowd, Drunken Boat, The Drunken Boat, Euphony, Exquisite Corpse, Five Points, Fortune, Good Foot, Hanging Loose, Ignition, Jacket, Jahrbuch der Lyrik 2002, Lineup, Nerve, The New Republic, The Paris Review, Pharos, Pif, Pleiades, Ploughshares, Shiny, Slate, Sundog, Tin House, Urbanus, Washington Square, Western Humanities Review, Word Virtual.com.* A few dates had to be changed in cases where more than one poem worth saving was written on the same month and day.

My thanks to Mark Bibbins, Denise Duhamel, Amy Gerstler, Glen Hartley, Stacey Harwood, Rachel Sussman, and Paul Violi for reading versions of this manuscript and suggesting changes for strengthening it. I owe a special debt to Gillian Blake, my editor at Scribner, for her enthusiasm and her acumen.